LEAVES FROM THE TREE OF PEACE

A Resource Book of Words and Pictures

Edited by
JOHN P REARDON

"the leaves of the tree serve for the
healing of the nations." *Revelation 22.2.*

The United Reformed Church ©
86 Tavistock Place London WC1H 9RT

1986

1.

A mark of true humanity is to be sensitive to beauty. The glory of God is reflected in the order of the universe, in the majesty and terror of great immensities, in variety of light and colour and sound, in the charm which the bodies of living things can display. Mankind's response to its physical environment in the form of work can be graced with elegance and distinction where, in the form of play, there is added response which creates and reveals beauty. The enjoyment of beauty, especially if unrelated to all that makes for human well-being, can blind men to God even in their appreciation of the beauty he makes possible; the inordinate pursuit of beauty may close their lives to other aspects of his call upon them. But where beauty is wantonly neglected or destroyed, the world is impoverished and God's purpose is dishonoured.

A Declaration of Faith – The Congregational Church in England and Wales.

2.

Peace is like gossamer –
vulnerable, yet indestructible:
tear it, and it will be rewoven.
Peace does not despair.
Begin to weave a web of peace:
start in the centre
and make peace with yourself
and your God.
Take the thread outwards
and build peace within your family, your community
– and in the circle of those you find it hard to like.
Then stretch your concern
into all the world.
Weave a web of peace
and do not despair.
Love is the warp in the fabric of life:
truth is the weft:
care and integrity together –
vulnerable,
but ultimately
indestructible.
Together,
they spell
peace...

Kate Compston

3.

I seek for peace – I care not where 'tis found:
On this rude scene in briers and brambles drest,
If peace dwells here, 'tis consecrated ground,
And owns the power to give my bosom rest;
To soothe the rankling of each bitter wound,
Gall'd by rude envy's adder-biting jest,
And worldly strife – ah, I am looking round
For peace's hermitage, can it be found?
Surely that breeze that o'er the blue wave curl'd
Did whisper soft, 'Thy wanderings here are blest.'
How different from the language of the world!
Nor jeers nor taunts in this still spot are given:
Its calm's a balsam to a soul distrest;
And, where peace smiles, a wilderness is heaven.

John Clare

4.

In weighing the fate of the earth
and, with it, our own fate,
we stand before a mystery,
and in tampering with the earth
we tamper with a mystery.
We are in deep ignorance.
Our ignorance should dispose us to wonder,
our wonder should make us humble,
our humility should inspire us to
reverence and caution,
and our reverence and caution
should lead us to act without delay
to withdraw the threat we now pose
to the earth and to ourselves.

Jonathan Schell 'The Fate of the Earth'

5.

Teach your children
what we have taught our children,
that the earth is our mother.
Whatever befalls the earth
befalls the sons of the earth.
If men spit upon the ground,
they spit upon themselves.

This we know.
The earth does not belong to man;
man belongs to earth.
This we know.
All things are connected
like the blood
which unites one family.

All things are connected.

Whatever befalls the earth
befalls the sons of the earth.
Man did not weave the web of life,
he is merely a strand in it.
Whatever he does to the web,
he does to himself.

Chief Seattle

6.

Whilst in Rome this summer, we visited the Colosseum. This was the scene of great barbarism and cruelty; the site, not only of the slaughter of thousands of animals 'for sport', but of the first martyring of Christians. While looking at the ruins, we saw a little cat prancing about in the tunnels where animals of old had been kept before coming out to be killed...

Colosseum

Little cat
springing among the tufted grass –
(nature's kindly carpet
on man's atrocities) –
have you not heard?
can you not smell the blood?
nor sense fear's protest
tolling in the stones?
They say at Auschwitz
no birds sing:
Should you not so decline
to walk and claim your scraps
in this round hell of hurt?

The years have been
too many; and the sun
has bleached the stones all white again,
and rain washed out the memories.
A thousand years from now, perhaps,
the birds will sing once more
in last night's Colosseum;
and nature will forgive
the cruelty of man –
and cats spring through the grasses on the graves.

Kate Compston

7.

The love God has for us

Dear friends, let us love one another, because love is from God. Everyone who loves is a child of God and knows God, but the unloving know nothing of God. For God is love; and his love was disclosed to us in this, that he sent his only Son into the world to bring us life. The love I speak of is not our love for God, but the love he showed to us in sending his Son as the remedy for the defilement of our sins. If God thus loved us, dear friends, we in turn are bound to love one another. Though God has never been seen by any man, God himself dwells in us if we love one another; his love is brought to perfection within us.

1 John 4. 7-12

8.

Let us throw up our caps in the sunlight,
    Let us welcome the Prince we adore;
But let us remember there's one light,
    Our Emperor cannot restore:–
The light of young lives just departed
    The light of love lost in the grave,
Past joys to the now broken-hearted,
    The light of the souls of the brave...

Mary Elizabeth Braddon 1859

9.

Waste

Waste of Muscle, waste of Brain,
Waste of Patience, waste of Pain,
Waste of Manhood, waste of Health,
Waste of Beauty, waste of Wealth,
Waste of Blood, and waste of Tears,
Waste of Youth's most precious years,
Waste of ways the Saints have trod,
Waste of Glory, waste of God, –
    War!

G A Studdert Kennedy

10.

... All that pretend to fight for Christ, are deceived; for his kingdom is not of this world, therefore his servants do not fight. Fighters are not of Christ's kingdom, but are without Christ's kingdom; his kingdom starts in peace and righteousness, but fighters are in the lust, and all that would destroy men's lives, are not of Christ's mind, who came to save men's lives. Christ's kingdom is not of this world; it is peaceable; and all that are in strife, are not of his kingdom.

George Fox from his Journal

11.

The world has a choice. It can continue to pursue the arms race, or it can move with deliberate speed towards a more sustainable international economic and political order.

It cannot do both.

Clyde Sanger 'Safe and Sound'

12.

We must repent

Just War Christians have been... unfaithful to the
best insights of their tradition. Instead of holding
up an explicit standard by which believers could
measure the policies of their governments, they
have unabashedly lapsed into using the 'just war'
as a slogan. Our country always fights just wars;
our means are invariably just and necessary.
(Our Christian enemies, viewing the same wars
from their perspective, have generally viewed
their causes and means as equally just. The most
recent example of this is the Argentinians of
1982). As technology has enabled warfare to
become increasingly destructive and indis-
criminate, Just War adherents have seldom
expressed their disapproval. Accustomed to
being good citizens, Christians in the Just
War tradition have been unaccustomed to
saying 'no'. Instead of withdrawing like many
pacifists into purist irrelevance, Just War
Christians have been 'relevant' at the price of
saying nothing of substance.

*From 'Time to Choose' Celebration Services (Post Green)
Ltd 1983.*

13.

We hear the cries of millions who face a daily
struggle for survival, who are crushed by military
power or the propaganda of the powerful. We
see the camps of refugees and the tears of all
who suffer human loss. We sense the fear of rich
groups and nations and the hopelessness of
many in the world rich in things who live in great
emptiness of spirit. There is a great divide
between North and South, between East and
West. Our world – God's world – has to choose
between "life and death, blessing and curse".

*'Gathered for Life' Report of the VI Assembly of the World
Council of Churches 1983.*

14.

Throughout the Bible God appears as the liber-
ator of the oppressed. He is not neutral. He does
not attempt to reconcile Moses and Pharaoh, to
reconcile the Hebrew slaves with their Egyptian
oppressors or to reconcile the Jewish people
with any of their later oppressors. Oppression is
sin and it cannot be compromised with, it must
be done away with. God takes sides with the
oppressed. As we read in Psalm 103:6 (JB) "God
who does what is right, is always on the side of
the oppressed".

From the Kairos Document from South Africa.

15.

First they came for the Jews and I did not speak
out – because I was not a Jew.

Then they came for the communists and I did not
speak out – because I was not a communist.

Then they came for the trade unionists and I did
not speak out – because I was not a trade union-
ist.

Then they came for me – and there was no one
left to speak out for me.

Pastor Niemoeller

16.

Jesus died for justice rooted in love. He died for
justice rooted in the nature of God. He died for
the incomparable value of the individual person,
derived from the human capacity for relationship
with other persons and with God which is what
we mean by the "image of God". He died to save
that image, that capacity for relationship, from
defacement, either by the self-induced distortion
of sin or the dehumanization of being sinned
against. He died to restore the freedom and
responsibility which is the necessary condition
for love.

There are many people committed to the
struggle for freedom and justice without this
reference to God. We must both welcome and
admire their devotion. But without any superior
condescension towards them, we must hold fast
to the reference to God not merely as a pious
option but as the essential mainspring of our
struggle. For Jesus it was all rooted in his knowledge of the nature of God, and it must be so for
us. So far from being a distraction or a softening
of our effort, the Christian perspective is a unique
source of realism. It saves us from a sentimental
idealization of justice.

John V Taylor 'Weep Not For Me'

17.

Is not this what I require of you as a fast:
    to loose the fetters of injustice,
    to untie the knots of the yoke,
      to snap every yoke
    and set free those who have been crushed?
Is it not sharing your food with the hungry,
taking the homeless poor into your house,
    clothing the naked when you meet them
    and never evading a duty to your kinsfolk?

Isaiah 58. 6 – 7

Peace will not prevail unless people are actively involved.

18.

The Dove

One olive tree above the flood
and one branch is the sign
of solid land again.
You bring hope, messenger of peace.

What olive leaves do we discover
in the world's flood of pain?

The fall of a dictator,
a pact between old enemies,
a government halving its spending on arms,
a family embracing different cultures,
a doctor's care in a war-torn land,
and children with uncorrupted eyes.

Jesus of the olive grove
you knew the agony of doubt.
Shall we be saved?
Yes, in the garden dawn;
Yes, in the upper room
and yes, where the tree of life
bears leaves to heal the nations.

Bernard Thorogood

19.

We renew our commitment to justice and peace. Since Jesus Christ healed and challenged the whole of life, so we are called to serve the life of all. We see God's good gift battered by the powers of death. Injustice denies God's gifts of unity, sharing and responsibility. When nations, groups and systems hold the power of deciding other people's lives, they love that power. God's way is to share power, to give it to every person. Injustice corrupts the powerful and disfigures the powerless. Poverty, continual and hopeless, is the fate of millions; stolen land is a cause of bitterness and war; the diversity of race becomes the evil imprisonment of racism. We urgently need a new international economic order in which power is shared, not grasped. We are committed to work for it. But the question comes back to us, what of the Church? Do we yet share power freely? Do we cling to the wealth of the Church? Do we claim the powerful as friends and remain deaf to the powerless? We have tasks near home.

Injustice, flagrant, constant and oppressive, leads to violence. Today life is threatened by war, the increase in armaments of all sorts, and particularly the nuclear arms race. Science and technology, which can do so much to feed, clothe and house all people, can today be used to terminate the life of the earth. The arms race everywhere consumes great resources that are desperately needed to support human life. Those who threaten with military might are dealing in the politics of death. It is a time of crisis for us all. We stand in solidarity across the world to call persistently, in every forum, for a halt to the arms race. The life which is God's good gift must be guarded when national security becomes the excuse for arrogant militarism. The tree of peace has justice for its roots.

'Gathered for Life' Report of the VI Assembly of the World Council of Churches 1983.

*Children whose livelihood is scavenging for
rubbish in Bacolod City, Philippines.*

Justice and peace go together,
but the world is filled with so many injustices.

20.

Today or Any Day

Today
or any day

today or any day
the clouds are low and
the thin rain falling

falling on the sodden garden
of heavy flowers bent down
down with the weight of it

the flowers bent down
down with the weight of
the ache in the human heart

the human heart torn
by the years' sorrow and
pictures of starving children

of starving children in
a dry land
dry land where no rain

falls
never falls
today

today
or any day

K W Wadsworth

21.

How then are we to respond today to the plight of
Africa where 30 million people are on the verge
of starvation? This happens in a world where
there is more than enough food produced for
every man, woman and child to enjoy three full
meals every day with plenty to spare. Despite
this, 750 million people at the very least, will lie
hungry in their beds tonight. But, set this against
the fact that last year, unbelievably, 1.3 million
tons of food was destroyed in Europe. There is
surely a moral imperative to bring sanity to this
crazy and deadly situation, to restore human
dignity, to promote development and the
possibility of peace. We must look at ourselves
and our lifestyles. We must examine and change
the processes and structures of the world which
at present promote division and ultimately bring
death. We must turn them into mechanisms of
international collaboration and human solidarity,
and ultimately into sources of life.

Cardinal Basil Hume

22.

Even the most powerful Third World countries
feel insecure in a world of global tension and
local conflict, caused by border disputes and
other animosities. Their security is threatened by
poverty and deprivation, by economic inequality.
Many countries look increasingly to armaments —
usually imported from developed countries — as
a means of trying to defend their security. Yet
this diverts resources from economic development and further reduces security. There are
moreover some 62 states with populations of less
than one million, of which 36 have less than
200,000 inhabitants. They are vulnerable, and
cannot possibly afford to build up military
strength.

The principle of common security applies with
great force to Third World countries. Like the
countries which live in the presence of nuclear
weapons, they cannot achieve security against
their adversaries. They too must find political and
economic security through a commitment to joint
survival.

Common Security: A Programme for Disarmament

23.

O God of justice, hear our plea
And call us to community.
Without Your healing, we are torn.
Held in Your love, we are re-born.

You call to peace. We quarrel still.
In our mistrust, we fail Your will.
O save us in this crucial hour,
Great God of justice, peace, and power.

Teach us that peace is meant to be
A way of life for all to see.
That friend and foe alike be shown
Redeeming love through us made known.

God, may the day envisioned come
When justice, peace, and joy for some
Shall be for all, not just a few,
Your reign in mercy coming true.

Jane Parker Huber
Sung to the tune Maryton

24.

O God, to those who have hunger give bread;
and to us who have bread
give the hunger for justice.

Latin American prayer

From chaos and fear there must be change,
leading to growth, development and a more
peaceful world.

25.

The Weight of a Snowflake

"Tell me the weight of a snowflake," a coalmouse asked a wild dove.

"Nothing more than nothing," was the answer.

"In that case, I must tell you a marvellous story," the coalmouse said.

"I sat on the branch of a fir, close to its trunk, when it began to snow – not heavily, not in a raging blizzard: no, just like in a dream, without a sound and without any violence. Since I did not have anything better to do, I counted the snowflakes settling on the twigs and needles of my branch. Their number was exactly 3, 741, 952. When the 3, 741, 953rd dropped onto the branch – nothing more than nothing, as you say – the branch broke off".

Having said that, the coalmouse flew away.

The dove, since Noah's time an authority on the matter, thought about the story for a while, and finally said to herself: "Perhaps there is only one person's voice lacking for peace to come to the world".

From 'New Fables, Thus spoke the Marabou' by Kurt Kauter.

26.

Peace

Forgive us, Lord, the selfishness
  That breaks your peace:
The wounded pride, the jealousy
  That finds release
    In shattering others' calm.

Forgive us, Lord, the empty prayer
  For peace on earth,
So loudly spoke, so little felt;
  We shrink the birth
    Of Christlike sympathy.

Forgive us, Lord, the weakened will
  That rests content
At peace where justice is denied
  And lives are rent
    By inhumanity.

Lord, give us now the inner peace
  For which we pray,
And by your love give strength of mind
  To win a day
    When all are reconciled.

Stephen Orchard

27.

A Prayer

Father of all people, we pray for the poor:
  homeless people seeking shelter,
  unemployed people wanting work,
  hungry people foraging for food,
  mothers crying for their children,
  refugees fleeing in fear.

We know that their poverty is a rebuke to us all,
  for they are at the bottom of the world's priorities,
  they cannot make decisions about their future,
  they are victims of other people's greed and neglect.

Awaken us to a sense of outrage and a spirit of compassion;
  show us how to engage in the struggle of the poor for an end to injustice,
  for a new world, one world,
  in which all your people
  will have the basic needs
  for a full and fulfilling life.

John Reardon

28.

The Grace of Touch

The Sistine touch gave life, the vital spark
Across the void to Adam. But in light or dark
We feel the touch, not coolly held in paint,
Which, known, confirms our being, sinner, fool and saint.
        Touch of your hand.

Warm comfort when a mother holds a child,
Thrashing at night caught in a net of dreaming wild;
A touch the madman knew among the tombs
When Legion fled, leaving a mind of ordered rooms.
        Touch of your hand.

The surgeon's touch, guiding the glinting steel,
Reaches the heart of pain to cauterise and heal
The inner sore. A therapeutic cut
The temple feels, excising cancer from the gut.
        Touch of your hand.

Untouchable the leper sees the crowd
Withdraw, until a Francis in delight declares he's proud
To run his hand across the noduled face,
And clasp our brother leper in a hug of grace.
        Touch of your hand.

Knowledge and love our fingers sensitise,
But rarely do we wait to feel with lovers' eyes.
And when like Thomas doubting you I stand
You will reach out, across this crowded no-man's land,
        To touch my hand.

Bernard Thorogood

29.

Prayer

Living Lord, in a dark hour
you spoke of the gift of peace;
we beg that gift for ourselves
that we may have the inner serenity
that cannot be taken from us
that we may become messengers of peace
to a strife torn world.

Edmund Banyard

30.

To follow Jesus
is to be a peacemaker.
The idea is spreading.
And the government
is worried.

Jim Wallis

31.

A new century nears, and with it the prospects of a new civilisation. Could we not begin to lay the basis for that new community with reasonable relations among all people and nations, and to build a world in which sharing, justice, freedom, and peace might prevail?

Willy Brandt in 'Common Crisis'

32.

There can be no hope of victory in a nuclear war, the two sides would be united in suffering and destruction. They can survive only together. They must achieve security not against the adversary but together with him. International security must rest on a commitment to joint survival rather than on a threat of mutual destruction.

Common Security: A Programme for Disarmament

A diverse humanity under the divine hand of God.

*A young witness for peace at a church conference
and festival in Kaiserslautern, West Germany, 1982.*

33.

Oh, war! What infamy, shame, and sorrow! War! What theft and crime, abetted, forgiven and glorified!

Recently I visited a large steel works. I will not say in what country, for all countries have been hospitable to me, and I am neither a spy nor a traitress. I only set forth things as I see them. Well, I visited one of these frightful manufactories, in which the most deadly weapons are made. The owner of it all, a multi-millionaire, was introduced to me. He was pleasant, but no good at conversation, and he had a dreamy, dissatisfied look. My cicerone informed me that this man had just lost a huge sum of money, nearly sixty million francs.

'Good Heavens!' I exclaimed; 'how has he lost it?'

'Oh well, he has not exactly lost the money, but has just missed making the sum, so it amounts to the same thing.'

I looked perplexed, and he added, 'Yes; you remember that there was a great deal of talk about war between France and Germany with regard to the Morocco affair?'

'Yes.'

'Well, this prince of the steel trade expected to sell cannon for it, and for a month his men were very busy in the factory working day and night. He gave enormous bribes to influential members of the Government and paid some of the papers in France and Germany to stir up the people. Everything has fallen through, thanks to the intervention of men who are wise and humanitarian. The consequence is that this millionaire is in despair. He has lost sixty or perhaps a hundred million francs.'

I looked at the wretched man with contempt, and I wished heartily that he could be suffocated with his millions, as remorse was no doubt utterly unknown to him.

And how many others merit our contempt just as this man does! Nearly all those who are known as 'suppliers to the army', in every country in the world, are the most desperate propagators of war.

Sarah Bernhardt 'My Double Life'

35.

When the World Alliance of Reformed Churches met in Ottawa last August (1982), we spent considerable time discussing a statement on peace. During the debate, a delegate from Africa made a remark that very poignantly raised some of the tensions surrounding this issue in the ecumenical movement today. He said: "In this document, the word 'nuclear' is used a number of times, but I don't ever see the word 'hunger'. In my village, the people will not understand the word 'nuclear', but they know everything about hunger and poverty."

What he was really talking about was the concern of many Christians in the "third world" that the issue of peace will be separated from the issue of justice, making of peace primarily a North Atlantic concern. This should not happen. First of all because ideologies of militarism and national security are international in character and cause deprivation and the continuation of injustice everywhere, but especially in the so-called "third world" countries. But secondly, and more importantly, in the Bible peace and justice are never separated. Peace is never simply the absence of war, it is the active presence of justice. It has to do with human fulfilment, with liberation, with wholeness, with a meaningful life and wellbeing, not only for the individual, but for the community as a whole. And the prophet Isaiah speaks of peace as the offspring of justice.

Allan Boesak

36.

In many countries, including the poorest arms-importing countries in Africa, even the 'civilian-type' goods and services which are produced locally in developed countries must be imported: such countries import uniforms and army boots, and even construction materials and technicians for building simple military facilities. There is little possibility that military production will stimulate economic growth in these countries.

Common Security: A Programme for Disarmament

34.

'Every gun that is made, every warship that is launched, every rocket fired signifies a theft from those that hunger and are not fed, from those who are cold and are not clothed.'

President Eisenhower

37.

Pilgrimage of Peace

Peace is not the journey's end
but the journey's making.
It is the struggle to be free,
response to hunger's cry;
walking with the derelict
and hearing the oppressed.

Peace is not the idling on still waters
but riding out the storm,
braving the wide ocean,
charting unknown seas,
throwing the life-line to the drowning
from the ship that foundered on the rocks.

Peace is not a dream of unrealised hopes;
it is running for the prize;
it is training to attain,
accepting the cost of following,
being ready for the sacrifice and pain;
it is the faith that dares to find a way.

Peace is not the false prophet's haven of rest.
It is the challenge of the Prince of peace;
the calling from the God of peace;
fruit of abiding in the Spirit of peace.
It is responding to the call of Christ
to announce good news, the gospel of peace.

John Johansen-Berg

38.

I am a man of peace. I believe in peace. But I do
not want peace at any price. I do not want the
peace that you find in stone; I do not want the
peace that you find in the grave; but I do want the
peace which you find embedded in the human
breast, which is exposed to the arrows of the
whole world, but which is protected from all harm
by the power of Almighty God.

Mahatma Gandhi

40.

Someday,
after mastering
the winds, the waves,
the tides and gravity,
we shall harness for God
the energies of love,

and then,
for the second time
in the history of the world,
man will discover fire.

Teilhard de Chardin

41.

A Prayer

Lord,
when we pray for peace,
show us again and again,
that there can be no peace
without the establishment of justice,
and the renewal of integrity.

When we are tempted to retreat
into a sentimental peace of mind,
stir within us
the passion for justice which Amos had,
the social vision of Isaiah,
the international courage of Jeremiah,
and the personal responsibility of Hosea.

Then, Lord,
within the struggle,
for righteousness and equality,
for wholeness and honesty,
come to us with that special greeting
which you alone can provide,
dispelling our eternal fears,
cancelling our guilt,
refreshing our spirits:
the welcome, the peace, of your son,
Jesus Christ,
our Risen Lord.

David Jenkins

39.

By three things is the world preserved: By truth
                                            By judgement
                                            And by peace

Authorised Daily Prayer Book, United Hebrew Congregation

Peace march with 90,000 people during the Kirchentag in Hanover, West Germany, 1983.

42.

Shun Hatred

How easily The Cause
becomes the God,
the shadow under which we hide
in blinkered safety.
    How easily, because we serve The Cause
    with sacrifice, we think, in various ways,
    and parrot-like repeat its slogans to ourselves,
    we pride ourselves, like pious Pharisees
    whose orthodoxy is beyond all doubt.
        How can we work for peace
        when there is pride and enmity within,
        if anger blinds us so we cannot see
        the good in others.
        This is hard.
            It takes a saint to bless the one opposed to him,
            especially if that opposition rules with mindless power.
            It's hard
            to love the sinner, though one hates the sin,
            to love the heretic, yet hate the lie,
            to love the enemy, and wish him good, yet stand
                foursquare against his charge.
            Only a saint does that.
            And yet the wisdom of the saints speaks clear;
                SHUN HATRED.
            because the hatred in your heart
            will wreck your cause,
                your argument,
                yourself.

Basil E Bridge

43.

The beginning of the 1980s has brought an unprecedented international manifestation of concern about nuclear war and insecurity. It is of the greatest importance to maintain the momentum of this period, not to disappoint people's hopes and efforts, to transform their longing for peace into a policy for peace.

Common Security: A Programme for Disarmament

44.

To refuse to struggle against the evil of the world is to surrender your humanity; to struggle against the evil of the world with the weapons of the evil-doer is to enter into your humanity; to struggle against the evil of the world with the weapons of God is to enter into your divinity.

Mahatma Gandhi

45.

'Someday the demand for disarmament by hundreds of millions will, I hope, become so universal and so insistent that no man, no nations, can withstand it.'

President Eisenhower

A discordant, fierce world of weapons and missiles:
movement and change are needed for peace — the
action of the Holy Spirit.

46.

Full spring is a glorious time in temperate lands. The sun dares to be warm again in slowly lengthening days. The riot of colour of the spring flowers drives far away memories of the bleak mid-winter. Already summer's promise is advanced in the new growth of bushes, the green of the trees.

Yet in a way the miracle of spring happens earlier. When snow still lies on the ground and nights are frosty. When days are still short and winds catch the breath. It is in those times that suddenly under the trees the snowdrops or aconites appear. Two clear days with some sunshine, and buds appear which were not there before. People subtly change mood. The winter is finished, though it still causes them to wrap up in warm clothes when they go out. Spring is in the air.

These are days of spring like that, if we have eyes and ears to observe the signals.

John Poulton 'The Feast of Life'

47.

I still believe that people are really good at heart...

If I look into the heavens I think that it will all come out right,

and that peace and tranquility will return again.

Anne Frank

48.

There is only one way to kill a wrong idea. It is to
set forth a right idea. You cannot kill hatred and
violence by violence and hatred. You cannot
make men out of love with war by making more
effective war. Satan will not cast out Satan,
though he will certainly seek to persuade us that
he will, since of all his devices this has been
throughout the ages the most successful. To
make war in order to make peace! How beguiling
an idea!

A Maude Royden 'The Great Adventure: the Way to Peace'

49.

EDUCATION FOR PEACE IS

Learning to respect and value oneself
Learning to respect and value other people
Understanding and appreciating one's own
culture and traditions
Understanding and appreciating other people's
culture and traditions
Learning to deal constructively and creatively
with conflict
Learning skills in cooperation
A broadening of horizons towards the wider
world, yet in a way which helps people to deal
with everyday issues.

Norman Richardson

50.

God said, 'This is the sign of the covenant which I establish between
myself and you and every living creature with you, to endless generations:

My bow I set in the cloud, sign of the covenant between myself
and earth.
When I cloud the sky over the earth, the bow shall be seen in
the cloud.'   *Genesis 9. 12 – 14*

All humankind is one with a Creator God
caring for this one world.

51.

All that we are is the result of what we have thought: it is founded on our thoughts, it is made up of our thoughts. If a man speaks or acts with evil thought, pain follows him, as the wheel follows the foot of the ox that draws the carriage.

All that we are is the result of what we have thought: it is founded on our thoughts, it is made up of our thoughts. If a man speaks or acts a pure thought, happiness follows him, like a shadow that never leaves him.

'He abused me, he beat me, he defeated me, he robbed me' – in those who harbour such thoughts hatred will never cease.

For hatred does not cease by hatred at any time: hatred ceases by love – this is an old rule.

The world does not know that we must all come to an end here; but those who know it, their quarrels cease at once.

Gautama Buddha

52.

There is nothing that we want more than true reconciliation and genuine peace – the peace that God wants and not the peace the world wants (Jn 14:27). The peace that God wants is based upon truth, repentance, justice and love. The peace that the world offers us is a unity that compromises the truth, covers over injustice and oppression and is totally motivated by selfishness. At this stage, like Jesus, we must expose this false peace, confront our oppressors and sow dissension. As Christians we must say with Jesus: "Do you suppose that I am here to bring peace on earth. No, I tell you, but rather dissension" (Lk 12:51). There can be no real peace without justice and repentance.

It would be quite wrong to try to preserve 'peace' and 'unity' at all costs, even at the cost of truth and justice and, worse still, at the cost of thousands of young lives. As disciples of Jesus we should rather promote truth and justice and life at all costs, even at the cost of creating conflict, disunity and dissension along the way. To be truly biblical our Church leaders must adopt a theology that millions of Christians have already adopted – a biblical theology of direct confrontation with the forces of evil rather than a theology of reconciliation with sin and the devil.

From the Kairos Document from South Africa.

53.

A Hymn on Human Rights

For the healing of the nations,
Lord, we pray with one accord,
for a just and equal sharing
of the things that earth affords.
To a life of love in action
help us rise and pledge our word.

Lead us, Father, into freedom,
from despair your world release,
that redeemed from war and hatred
all may come and go in peace.
Show us how through care and goodness
fear will die and hope increase.

All that kills abundant living,
let it from the earth be banned:
pride of status, race or schooling,
dogmas that obscure your plan.
In our common quest for justice
may we hallow life's brief span.

You, Creator-God, have written
your great name on humankind;
for our growing in your likeness
bring the life of Christ to mind;
that by our response and service
earth its destiny may find.

Fred Kaan
Suggested tune: 'Westminster'

2. The prophet had a vision
    of a place where all would learn
    the ways of the Lord together,
    the truth of his word discern;
Hammer your swords...

3. The prophet had a vision
    of a day when all would find
    the end of war and bloodshed,
    the hope of humankind;
Hammer your swords...

4. The prophet had a vision
    of a world where all would share
    the bounty the Lord had given,
    and each for the other care;
Hammer your swords...

5. The prophet had a vision
    of the time we long for still,
    God's kingdom enfolding all men
    in peace as they do his will;
Hammer your swords...

Words and Music by Basil E Bridge

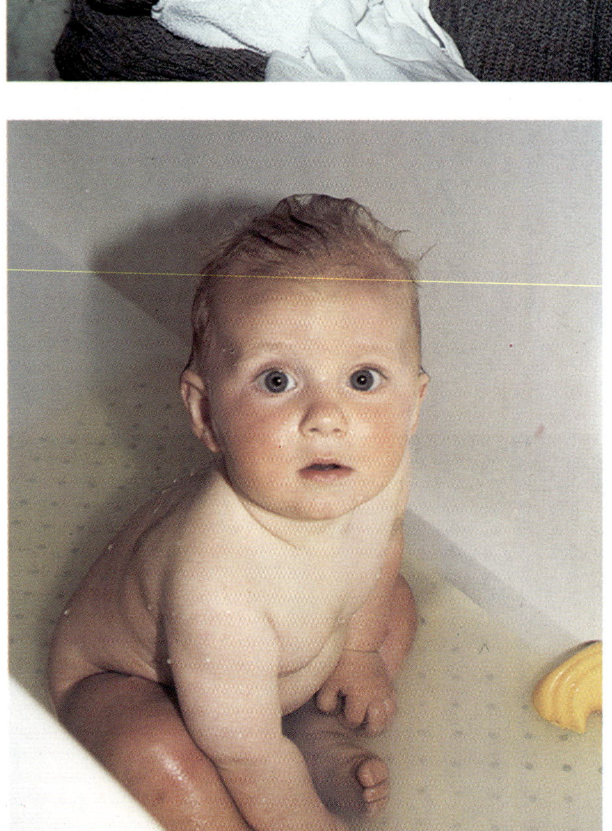

55. Voices For Peace

Tomorrow's children cannot plead
nor the long-suffering earth protest
against today's destroyers;
nor can our forbears cry,
whose sacrifice and toil,
whose vision and whose faith
helped to create the fragile good
that we today enjoy,
the fragile good
we could so easily destroy
either by fear, or folly, or mistake.
Only through those who see and care today
the past, the future, and the earth itself
can find a voice;
can plead for peace and life.
Dare we give them a voice to use?
Dare we refuse?

Basil E Bridge

56.

An Event in Asia and Shaker Heights

In an isolated event
Somewhere in Asia,
A boy twenty
Steps on a mine
And is instantly killed.

This sets in motion
A chain
That ends at the door
Of an apartment
In Shaker Heights,
Where an embarrassed soldier
Dressed in green
Must tell
A tremble-chinned lady
Gray curls flattened
To her head
With the man
Half bald behind her,
That all the years
Of care
For this human being
Carried under heart,
Through childhood
To adult
Have been obliterated.

Laurel Spear

57.

Christ, the life of the world, is our peace
(Eph. 2:14). Our hopes for a world where life is
not threatened by nuclear holocaust, or slow
starvation, for a world where justice and peace
embrace each other, are based in Jesus Christ,
the Crucified and Risen One who has triumphed
over the powers of evil and death, and therefore
will not allow the ultimate triumph of injustice and
war. True peace comes only from God, who can
turn even the wrath of man to God's praise
(Ps. 76:10). True peace is more than the
absence of war: it means restored relationships
of love, compassion and justice.

*'Gathered for Life' Report of the VI Assembly of the World
Council of Churches 1983.*

59.

Goodness is stronger than evil;
Love is stronger than hate;
Light is stronger than darkness;
Life is stronger than death;
Victory is ours through Him who loved us.

Desmond Tutu

60.

... Love will teach us all things: but we must learn
how to win love; it is got with difficulty: it is a
possession dearly bought with much labour and
in a long time; for one must love not sometimes
only, for a passing moment, but always. There is
no man who doth not sometimes love: even the
wicked can do that.

And let not men's sin dishearten thee: love a man
even in his sin, for that love is a likeness of the
divine love, and is the summit of love on earth.
Love all God's creation, both the whole and
every grain of sand. Love every leaf, every ray of
light. Love the animals, love the plants, love each
separate thing. If thou love each thing thou wilt
perceive the mystery of God in all; and when
once thou perceive this, thou wilt thenceforward
grow every day to a fuller understanding of it:
until thou come at last to love the whole world
with a love that will then be all-embracing and
universal.

Dostoevsky 'The Brothers Karamazov'

61.

A Prayer

In all our attitudes,
keep us humble, courageous and enterprising;
ready to face anger and persecution;
prepared for disappointment and frustration;
living always as those
who already possess your peace,
and by our delight in it,
making it real for the world.

Alan Gaunt

58.

But the harvest of the Spirit is love, joy, peace, patience,
kindness, goodness, fidelity, gentleness, and self-control.

Galatians 5. 22

62.

I do not hope for a world at peace, all of it, all the time. I do not believe in the perfectibility of man, which is what would be required for universal peace; I only believe in the human race. I believe that the human race must continue. Our leaders are not wise enough, nor brave enough, nor noble enough, for their jobs. We, the led, are largely either sheep or tigers; we are all guilty of stupidity, the ruling human sin. This being so, we can expect wars; we have never been free of them. I hate this fact and accept it.

But nuclear war is unlike any other kind of war that has threatened mankind, and cannot be thought of in the old known terms. Nuclear war reaches a dimension unseen before in history. That dimension is towering, maniacal conceit.

Martha Gellhorn 'The Face of War'

63.

More and more
of the decisions
which effect human lives
will be scientific decisions.

They must not be made
by persons who are not equipped
to understand
the moral consequences.

Dr Aaron Ihde

64.

Nuclear deterrence can never provide the foundation of genuine peace. It is the antithesis of an ultimate faith in that love which casts out fear. It escalates the arms race in a vain pursuit of stability. It ignores the economic, social and psychological dimensions of security, and frustrates justice by maintaining the status quo in world politics. It destroys the reality of self-determination for most nations in matters of their own safety and survival, and diverts resources from basic human needs.

'Gathered for Life' Report of the VI Assembly of the World Council of Churches 1983.

65.

Peace is not a monumental construction resting solidly on permanent foundations set firm in a given tract of ground. It much more resembles a seaworthy vessel navigating an uncertain sea, its safety at any moment depending on its ability to withstand, or adapt to, the vagaries of the weather, on the technical skill, unity of purpose and comradeship of the crew and on the experience and resourcefulness of the men on the bridge. Furthermore the voyage is perpetually into the unknown. No peace is lasting in the sense of being attainable once for all and thereafter taken for granted.

The Search for Security: Report of a British Council of Churches Working Party 1973.

66.

Prayer for Peace

Lead me from death to life,
from falsehood to truth.

Lead me from despair to hope,
from fear to trust.

Lead me from hate to love,
from war to peace.

Let peace fill our heart,
our world, our universe...